THE POEMS OF NEW REVELATION

AUTHOR JOEL MAX

Published by New Generation Publishing in 2023

First Edition

ISBN
Hardback	978-1-80369-747-5
eBook	978-1-80369-748-2

www.newgeneration-publishing.com

New Generation Publishing

Author Joel Max
U.S. Citizen
J.D. (Juris Doctor)
D. Min (Doctor of Ministry)
From U.S. institutions
Contact: monadhs639@gmail.com

CONTENTS

Preface 1

Prologue – The Grave 3

A Legend About Heart 7

A Legend About Greed 21

The Song of Revelation 40

A Legend About the Dead 52

The Genesis in a Dream 62

The Letters of God 89

The Lamentation of the East I 95

The Lamentation of the East II 115

The History of Gods I – The Sedona Mountain 133

The History of Gods II – The Sedona Mountain 143

The History of Gods III 148

The History of Gods IV 158

Epilogue - The Chosen Destiny 168

Preface

There have been countless revelations in human history. Nostradamus' prophetic poems and Seth's channeled messages are widely known among them. There are many other poems, songs, and other writings that reflect spiritual inspirations or revelations about the invisible world.

We all can hear sounds not heard in the physical and visible world if we listen to nature, the sound within, and things invisible. Poets write poems by listening to those inaudible sounds, like channelers or messengers.

As we can hear them only in silence and solitude, sometimes, reaching and maintaining the state in which we can hear such sounds may become a dark night of the soul.

Fourteen poems are contained in this collection. The author wrote these poems in the desert, paying attention to the inaudible stories and sounds that may reflect the breathing or lamentation of our age.

We live in an age where people are not interested in reading poems. AIs produce rhymes. In the desert, however, even a single dew may revive a dying life.

Each poem is born out of a particle of life. A life can come only from life.

Once born in this world, the poems will stay alive no matter how long it may take until they can be read by somebody. Waiting does not matter at all.

The author does not know who will meet these poems and when. It might take a hundred years to find a reader. The time and the number of readers will only be foliage. Sending blessings for any and all who will meet these poems.

Prologue – The Grave

It is Nighttime.

Light Appears to Exist

Nowhere.

The stars disappeared in the sky,

A long time ago.

Does time still exist in such darkness?

Am I alive or dead?

Not sure.

It might be nonsense,

To distinguish "alive" or "dead,"

Only with "breathing."

Will that morning come?

The morning

I have been waiting.

Has the morning ever existed?

Should I create it?

Countless signs of waiting

Are only seen,

In every corner of life.

My shape will not stay here for long.

Old garments will vanish,

As the fog disappears.

Some songs circle over my head

Like a pack of eagles

That gather for the smell of death,

For the traces of the dead,

Coming from the remaining scars,

Not replaced with the marks of the living.

It may even be a luxury,

To call the song of darkness

Brought out of the night,

"Vanity."

Living as a trap,

And as a prickly thorn,

For too many,

Created a night of darkness.

Who are you?

What is it?

The night is full of legends with lamentation.

I love the night.

The night,

Where I finally can find a trace of light.

A Legend About Heart

In the beginning, there was Heart,

Like a wooden box.

Nature from the earth was in it.

Man needed it to live.

In the beginning, there was Heart.

It was like a treasure chest.

The soul from above was in it.

It was like a breath or a spirit.

Divine power and nature were stored in it.

The soul needed it to live.

In the Garden of Eden, which vanished into the legend,

There was a road from Eden to Heaven

On the side of the road

Above the fire sword,

The tree of life was seen.

The time,

Death

Did not exist in the garden.

No hunger, no thirst, and no craving were there.

Humans, gods, and animals

fearlessly communicated with each other.

Transparent and crystal water

flow in the four valleys of the garden.

It was like a paradise.

Before the numbers appeared,

A spirit called Greed,

expelled from Heaven,

down to Eden

was united with a snake.

The snake planted the seed of Greed in humans.

The Greed

had many kinds of powers.

But simply,

It's craving something more than necessary,

King Solomon said,

it's a useless spirit,

Cause its origin is vanity.

Meanwhile,

Man worshiped it.

It became an idol soon.

The Greed,

Was escorted by anger, hatred, blame, and fear,

Always, from the beginning.

With that in mind,

It was sometimes called evil nature.

Heart tainted with Greed,

It was called corruption by old sages.

Some sages said,

Corruption is compared with the nature of animals.

Not necessarily.

Because animals do not hunt

When they are full.

Yet,

Humans with Greed never feel full.

They continue to hunt,

No matter how full they are,

And even when their storage

Has no space for more.

Some religions said,

It is the nature of a red dragon,

A symbol of evil used by them,

Which will vanish according to their prophecy.

From the time Humans followed Greed,

Without any necessity,

They kept feeling lacking.

Cause their senses, eyes, and ears,

Were all transformed,

In alignment with Greed.

Not only the feeling of lacking,

Humans with Greed

Heard Yes as No,

Saw other people's possessions as theirs.

They could not resist the craving of

Taking, possessing, and invading

Whatever was seen in their sight,

Whatever was heard in their ears,

And even the things that were not visible.

Those who could not resist a craving,

Chose to become God,

Not the original divinity within,

But the power controlling and invading others.

Humans who chose to be such God

Ate a fruit of good and evil.

It was their choice.

All choices have consequences.

Though it looked beautiful and tasty,

The fruit brought about their separation,

From the Creator,

From the original Heart,

The eyes of the humans who ate the fruit,

Became too brightening.

Yet, through the brightening eyes,

They saw things unreal,

Creating confusion and chaos,

In identifying the reality.

Illusion and delusion distorted reality.

In those twisted eyes,

Truth looked falsity,

Falsity looked true.

Beauty became shame,

Hatred was viewed as love,

Peace was called a coward.

Humans no longer loved the Garden of Eden.

They chose the way to the world of Greed.

Once Humans left the Garden of Eden,

They competed with each other to obtain things.

They began to fight with other humans,

Other villages, other nations, and the earth.

The divinity within disappeared.

The whole new world broke up,

Which was full of hostility, fear,

Incessant hunger and thirst,

Ruthless killing, looting, deceiving, and manipulation.

Humans taken by Greed have evolved this way.

Then, they created a military song,

Which scattered all over the place.

The song was sung in many different versions,

Although the essence of the meaning was the same.

"We have our own hands and feet.

Let's find the most propitious land.

Let's build a paradise better than Eden there.

We will build a wall that is so thick and so tall.

Gods will not invade the land.

Let's put a splendid flag showing the ownership,

The glorious human achievement,

Which will last forever."

A clay plate buried deep underneath the land,

shows the lives of humans after they departed Eden.

An anonymous author left a lamentation:

"On one side, the foundation work is done,

On the other side, stone cutting is done.

Some people burn the dirt for bricks,

Others keep boiling water,

While the dark dust from the place covers the sky.

Sunlight is blocked because of the dark dust and smoke.

Stars are not seen as the sky is covered with smoke.

Humans also lose the light in their hearts.

To build a paradise on earth,

Humans with weapons

Drag other humans,

Force them to work.

Locking them with chains,

Keeping whipping them for work productivity.

Both turn into monsters shortly.

In one corner,

The sound of singing and laughing is heard,

In the other corner,

The screams of resentment and hatred are listened to.

Under the thick darkness of the earth,

Each sound is scattered all over the place,

Merged with demons, ghosts, and phantoms,

Creating a city of madness.

The earth tries to alarm Humans,

Sometimes with volcanoes or earthquakes,

Other times, with floods or tornadoes.

Yet,

Humans cannot hear or see".

A Legend About Greed

A long, long time ago,

Before the great flood took place,

Greed ruled the human world.

The earth became dark.

Humans' hands and feet were chained,

Turning into slaves of Greed.

A group of sages appeared.

No one knew where they came from.

Some said,

Twelve stars in heaven

Came down to earth,

To repair the earth.

Others said,

They were angels from the sea.

Sages scattered across the ground.

When they tried to untie the chains

From the hands and feet of the slaves,

Greed stopped them,

Saying, "Unbridled freedom will cause great evil."

Passing by a castle encircled with tall walls,

Sages heard ghastly shrieks.

When they tried to tear down the walls,

Greed stopped them,

Saying, "They are being trained to become technicians."

Sages said,

"All humans are created equal.

Humans can't enslave other humans".

Then, Greed shut the sages' mouths up.

Saying," You are messing up the right of strongest."

Sages then tried to light up,

Hoping that the light would light up Humans.

Out of anger and fear,

Greed caught the sages,

Locked them up in the dark temple.

When mountains and fields were in commotion for the sages,

Greed whispered, "Sages do not like violence,"

Telling them to worship the sages in the temple,

With sacrificial animals.

The temple became a slaughterhouse,

Full of bloody smell and screams,

Yet

Greed called it a peace offering.

Sages left the temple,

Unknown to all.

Humans' appearances gradually changed,

Reflecting the darkness within.

They were no longer beautiful beings,

Running around the Garden of Eden,

Communicating with animals and gods

Fearlessly.

The fruits of Greed covered the earth.

Earth screamed,

Water screamed,

Mountains screamed,

In suffocation,

Crying for release,

Crying for restoration.

Suddenly,

Sky opened,

Water poured down from the sky,

Nonstop, for forty days,

Sweeping away the debris of corruption,

Clearing the fruits of Greed,

For a new beginning,

For restoration of the origin.

Time passed,

Water withered,

Living beings hidden

Appeared refreshed,

New thriving started.

Greed survived the Great Flood.

Greed started a new beginning.

Greed appeared as a God of wrath,

Judges, Kings, Scholars, and Sages.

With many more masks,

Greed always looked beautiful,

Sounded intelligent and profound.

Its speech was eloquent and logical.

Many began to worship,

Obey, praise, and envy Greed.

Seeking Greed's recognition,

Many created different gods,

As new fruits of Greed,

Worshipping them,

Seeking its favor.

Kingdoms were created,

Maintaining abodes of Greed.

Kings and Queens appeared,

Planting fear in the heart of man,

To control man,

Under the power of Greed.

Great and glorious kingdoms appeared,

With the presence of Greed.

Kings kept building walls,

Temples and palaces,

Searching for,

Collecting,

And storing gold and silver.

Through bloody wars,

Laborers and finances

Were supplied.

Laws were used,

For control, suppression,

And manipulation.

Through the creation of religion,

Kings and queens

Stole the heart of man,

Making man their puppet.

Countless gods' names

And their legends

Invisibly shackled Man's heart.

The smell of rotting bodies in the wilderness,

Made the wind exhausted from carrying the smell.

Countless unowned human bones

Were spread all over the ground.

Yet,

The kings who took out the sword,

Never knew how to put it back in the sheath.

Didn't they know their kingdoms would vanish?

Had they known it,

Would they have stopped using the names of gods,

For their victory in the bloody battlefields?

O, horse-riding Kings who took away other kingdoms,

What have you done with the kingdoms you had taken?

The great territory you had taken from others,

Where are they?

Where is the pioneer,

Who was destroyed invading other's land?

O, Rich! Power! Dragon!

O, Babylon,

You built an impregnable castle over a flowing river,

Singing a song of living a thousand years.

Where are all the gods in the temple now?

Where are all the kings in the palace now?

You piled up gold and silver,

Taken when unifying Sumer.

Where are they?

Were they eaten by mold?

Were they already rusty when you died?

Did you move them to the underworld?

What has swallowed the unified kingdom?

O, the Kingdom of Babylon,

You boasted your splendor and laws.

How come did you die that early?

O, Marduk,

Are you still playing God, in silence,

In the underworld?

O, Phoenician Kingdom,

You carved a monster form on the stone,

Calling it Molek,

Sacrificing babies captured,

To give him as burnt offerings.

Did Molek keep you safe forever?

Were you not afraid of the souls of burnt babies?

Did you only fear Molek?

Do you have beautiful graves on earth?

Are your precious bones kept safely,

Thanks to Molek?

O, Assyrian Kingdom,

You invaded others' territories,

Dragging young people,

Taking their eyes off,

Ripping their tongues out,

Peeling them off,

Hanging them on the wall,

In the name of cutting the buds of rebellion.

Their blood turned the water of the Euphrates into the blood.

Where is the beloved kingdom now?

Is there even a trace of your kingdom?

O, King Astyages,

You tried to kill your grandson,

Listening to a fortune teller,

To keep your throne.

Did you kill the baby?

Did you keep the throne?

O, Kingdom of Media,

You disappeared because of your king's illusion.

O, Great King Cyrus,

You were called the phoenix, born with heavenly luck.

You were thrown away in the wilderness,

As food for wild animals,

Right after birth.

Yet,

A cow keeper rescued you.

As the oracles foretold,

You became the great king,

Taking over your grandfather's kingdom.

Why didn't you stop there?

How come your craving for invasion didn't stop?

Had you stopped there,

Your neck would not have been cut by Tomiris.

Did you hear the words of Tomiris?

When she cut your neck and dip it in the blood,

She said,

"Drink blood as much as possible,

You bloodthirsty monster!"

Your heavenly luck which made you a phoenix,

Ended with misery,

As the fruit of Greed.

O, the Kingdoms built by humans and gods,

Jupiter! Zeus!

Oracle of Delphi!

O, Alexander the Great!

You never listened to the sages.

Where are your great kingdoms,

Palaces, and temples?

O, Egyptian Kingdom,

You controlled the flow of water,

Mastering the teachings of the star,

Knowing so many secrets of the universe.

You called the beasts of heaven,

Made them to be your guards,

And was aided by the snake with two heads.

Where are all those beasts?

Where is your great kingdom?

Where are those kings?

Where are those queens?

Where are those kingdoms?

Where are their precious children?

Where are their gold and silver?

Where are prophets for the kings?

Where are the gods created by them?

Where are the greatest emperors?

Who invaded the vast lands of the others?

All disappeared.

All are invisible.

Yet

Greed planted the seed of fear in man.

And, it planted,

The seed of control in

New kings and queens

Generation by generation,

Incessantly.

Some sages left their words,

On a plate buried in the deep earth.

The writing on the plate says,

"O, King! O, Kingdom! O, Emperor! O, Empire!

Put your sword in the sheath,

Stop horse riding,

Release a bridle of your horse,

Make him rest.

The smell of fragrance will return,

When the smell of blood disappears.

Then, your soil will become rich.

The soil you have ignored,

Is the secret of longevity.

The soil cannot be invaded by the angels of the dead."

The Song of Revelation

There was a man.

Running around mountains and fields,

Trying to catch the wind,

Figuring out the flow of the season,

Announcing that there is a season for everything.

The man said,

There is time for crying,

There is time for laughing.

People called him a wise man.

The wise man left his final word:

All is vanity.

Return to the Creator.

By doing the will of the Creator.

A sage came to the earth,

Made a clay plate,

Keeping it in his arms for a long time.

Then the sage recorded the meaning of the song

On the clay plate,

In Sumerian letters.

The song is a revelation about a secret,

About the world to come,

About the new heaven.

And about the new earth.

There was a great whore sitting on the fluctuating water.

Great kings slept with her.

Many others became drunk with her wine of fornication.

She rode a red beast of gold,

Her clothes were purple and red,

Adorned with jewels and pearls.

Gold cups were in her hands,

The gold cups were splendor,

But its inside was full of dirt.

On her forehead,

Her name was recorded:

Queen, Goddess.

Her place was full of amusement,

Some called it Sodom.

Some called it a Palace.

Her beauty, her splendor,

Her gold cups and her wine of fornication

Made many men drunk,

losing their consciousness.

Strong guards surrounded her.

Some called them beasts.

Some called them elites.

Some called them heroes.

One of the guards was riding a camel.

His speech was eloquent,

Full of logic.

He looked so intelligent and noble,

Some envied him.

His charm and intelligence were incomparable.

No truth could win him.

Another guard looked like a lion.

His voice sounded like a broken trumpet.

His eyes looked like the ones of a pig.

His appearance made people scared.

He gobbled others' food casually,

But nobody could resist.

He never listened to others,

Never saw others,

Never cared for others.

Anger and Greed were his weapons.

Another guard looked like a mudfish,

Escaping all traps.

It was too slippery and too thin to catch.

With his help.

Goddess and the other guards,

Could escape any trap safely.

He could steal others' things,

Unnoticed.

His smile eradicated suspicion.

With this talent,

He kept stealing others' things,

Escaped and ran away undetected.

When noticed,

Nobody could catch him.

He was too slippery to catch.

He could transform falsity into truth.

People could not see the falsity in him,

Because of his talent and smile.

Aided by these guards,

The Lady of Babylon

Kept killing, stealing, and torturing

Humans, animals, hearts, and minds.

Her storage was too full to store more.

She continued to stock items,

While they were getting rotten in the corners.

The young, the weak, and the poor cried.

The dead and tortured screamed.

The abandoned with scars grieved in pain.

The road was full of the hungry and the thirsty.

Is it hell?

The screams of people accumulated,

Reaching heaven,

Filling the ocean,

And covering the earth.

One day,

A layer covering the sunlight was removed,

Making the sunlight shiny and strong

All over the place on earth.

Then, all things on earth were shaken.

Things collapsed.

Beautiful flowers in her garden,

All died in black.

The gold and silver stored in her storage,

All became rusted.

The guards surrounding the Lady,

Vanished in the frost.

All she possessed also vanished.

All who fornicated with her,

Vanished into the air.

Is this the end of the time?

Is this the day of judgment?

All are shaken.

All are collapsed.

All vanished.

All are rotten,

All the happy faces are gone,

The rich and the kings vanished.

A sage appeared and said:

Behold,

The stage disappeared.

All players with costumes vanished.

The sage declared "Emancipation."

It is the day of restoration.

It is the time of the new creation.

A proclamation of restoration is heard.

Repentance is activated with

Complete and radical change.

The weak, the meek, and the young

Came out of the long and dark tunnel.

No more tears,

No more tortures,

No hunger and no thirst.

All became transparent,

Truth revealed its origin.

The song of the wise man is fulfilled.

"Do to others whatever you would have them do to you,"

A Legend About the Dead

A young man was traveling a way to the afterlife.

Not far away from the departure,

He reached a crossroads.

He chose one of several,

Because it looked fancy and shiny.

Once he entered the road,

It became dark and quiet.

He kept walking full of curiosity.

Suddenly, he heard the sound of a quarrel.

A man just died, and his soul departed the body.

At the crossroad,

He chose the road because it looked shiny.

Once he stepped into the road,

Two messengers in black appeared

To take him to the destination of the road.

The messengers looked scary and intimidating.

Out of suspicion,

The man asked them if he was going to Heaven.

The messengers laughed and said, "No."

Having realized that he chose the wrong road,

The man refused to follow them,

Trying to go back to the crossroad.

Stopping him from going back,

The messengers said that

Everybody chooses the road to take

Based on his own sight,

The fruit of his life on earth.

The man argued,

"Do you know who I am?

There should be an error.

I am the one who lived for God for life,

A pastor for a big church.

Thousands of people followed me.

I don't have sins

Because every sin of mine, if any,

Has been washed out by the blood of Jesus.

I drove out ghosts from people

In the name of Jesus.

I performed miracles through praying.

When I prayed for people,

My prayer was answered,

Messengers laughed.

Suddenly,

A film depicting each moment of his life

Was played like a flash.

Although it quickly disappeared,

Countless moments were depicted.

At each moment,

The man cruelly rejected, scolded, mocked, and cursed

The hungry, the thirsty, the sick, the imprisoned, and the weak.

His dark color heart was also shown transparently.

Somehow and momentarily,

A few phrases transpired to the viewers,

"No mercy for others,

Endless greed only for your children

At the expense of others,

No truth in heart,

Whole life with a mask."

When the film disappeared,

Suddenly and strangely,

The man's face became dark,

He became furious and violent,

Cursing the messengers and God in rage,

Trying to kill the messengers.

The Messengers stopped him

And took him by force toward the destination.

From somewhere,

Somebody sang,

"Birds of a feather flock together.

Surely,

People choose a road

Which matches their lives on earth.

No mistake, no error."

The young traveler returned to the crossroad.

Then he entered another road

Which looked like the countryside on earth.

Once entered the road,

The traveler could feel the fragrance of flowers.

Very soon,

He saw an open wagon,

Decorated with beautiful flowers,

Moving very slowly,

Escorted by four angels.

There was a light in the sky,

The road was full of exotic flowers.

Birds were singing joyfully.

A man was sitting in the wagon,

Chatting with angels.

The man was saying,

"Is it a dream? Why I am in this flower wagon?

Where am I going?"

The angels answered,

"You are in Heaven,

You will see God."

Being surprised,

The man said,

"This might be an error.

I have not done anything good."

The angels smiled.

Suddenly,

A film was played in the air,

Depicting countless moments of his life,

Showing his heart transparently.

Each moment,

He cared for others as if he was treating himself.

His heart was exactly the same as his face.

He said only the truth,

He did not use others for himself or his children.

He was generous in sharing what he had,

And understanding others.

He did not have anything to forgive,

Because he readily released others for their wrongs.

He was diligent in using what he had

All day and all his life,

Trying to use what he had,

Equally for his happiness

And for the happiness of others.

After the film disappeared,

A song was heard from above.

"Blessed are the merciful: for they shall obtain mercy.

Blessed are the pure in heart: for they shall see God."

The Genesis in a Dream

One day,

I had a long dream.

In the dream, I saw how the universe was created,

And the humans and the earth.

Before the beginning

Creator,

Made appear,

Hot and an invisible tiny particle.

It contained life, time, space,

The sun, moon, stars, and all elements,

The source of all things.

People later called it Big Bang,

Because it exploded and expanded

Instantly, rapidly, and constantly.

All things were in one.

One was all things.

All came together.

It was before the sun existed,

Light and darkness appeared.

The newborn beings

Began expansion at a lightning speed.

The expansion was called growth.

In the universe created,

Light appeared,

Darkness was recognized,

Nothingness was also cognized.

Life and death

Appeared as a cycle.

As the flow of time was created,

It was called "Frank's time."

The glaring fires gave birth,

Protons and neutrons,

They combined to birth atoms,

Atoms gave birth to hydrogen and helium,

They formed collectively 'Dust.'

The name of the earth is earth.

Science says it's the stuff of all things.

The elements and materials

Moved and blended,

According to the laws.

Gravity was one of them.

Words of the Creator

Resulting in the manifestation of all things,

Under the laws.

Once born,

The things that were created were named.

Just like a fetus grows in the womb,

The particles, the hot elements,

Spin and spin

Conglomerate and split,

Again and again,

Until they form a new creation,

As the form of the sun, moon, and stars,

All are according to the law.

Sun attracts its own groups,

Forming its own world.

People later called it the solar system.

Stars and planets gather together,

Creating huge groups.

The galaxies were thus created,

And are being created.

Earth is the third planet in the solar system.

All other planets were born and moving,

According to the law,

Keeping their positions,

Also evolving constantly.

Each one was unique,

Yet, each one was in harmony with the others,

Under the law,

Repeating creation, evolution, extinction, and new birth.

The Earth was thus born,

Within the solar system.

Substances were gathered by gravity,

Forming a tremendous fireball.

It was an infant earth.

The infant earth was blazing,

Absorbing various substances,

And growing in its size.

Suddenly,

An anonymous plat flew into the earth,

Resulting in a massive crash.

By the crash,

Some materials were ripped out of the earth.

The axis of rotation tilts,

Giving birth to seasons.

This axis of rotation is the center,

Which extends from its bottom to the top.

The axis, through rotation,

Created the day and the night.

Earth,

From the South pole to the North pole,

Generates energy,

And sends it toward the sun,

Creating the magnetic energy web in the atmosphere,

Blocking harmful dust from the solar wind,

With the magnetic field, a protective layer.

All things are in order.

Earth then experienced collisions,

With large and small ice planets.

Each time,

The blazing fireball was cooled,

Here and there,

Creating nucleus, internal and external,

As well as mantle and perception.

As it cooled,

The residuary water piled up,

As liquid and as solid substances.

Oxygen was born,

During the course,

According to the law of nature.

The water gave birth to a life.

Then, from the water,

The great continent rose,

Combined with stones, rocks, and soils,

People later called it Pangaea.

It was the first continent on earth.

According to the law of nature,

Set at the beginning,

The creatures appeared,

On the land that rose from the water.

Plants and trees of many kinds appeared.

Some creatures that were eating plants,

Also appeared in the form of males and females.

In the meantime,

The earth kept working,

For its own balance and its own growth,

With its portions being torn apart,

And conglomerating with other parts.

People later called it orogeny.

The change in perception,

And volcanic eruptions followed,

Producing enormous amounts of carbon dioxide.

Orogeny was to set the balance of all things on earth

This exercise,

After a long time

It formed the Appalachian Mountains in North America,

And the Hercynian Mountains in Europe and Asia.

During this course,

Here and there,

This time and that time,

The creatures were born,

in the water and land,

Repeating birth and death.

One time,

Suddenly,

So many living creatures appeared,

In the sea and on the land.

It was called the Cambrian explosion,

As the appearance of living creatures

Arose explosively.

Following the cycle of life and death,

As time goes by,

The creatures,

Went into the vanishing world,

Earth experienced at least five extinction events.

At first, in the Paleozoic Ordovician--Silurian period,

And then, in the Devonian Period of the Paleozoic Era.

More extinction events occurred,

Including the well-known one during which

All dinosaurs were extinct.

After the series of cycles of birth and death,

Still, many years ago, in human numbers,

Over six hundred thousand years ago,

One meteorite fell on the earth.

It was in the area now known as Yucatan Peninsula.

This ended the Mesozoic Age,

The crash left an enormous mark on the earth,

Causing particles, dusted fog,

To cover the sky,

Blocking the sunshine from the earth.

The earth turned into a dark world.

Plants and microbes died,

As they could no longer do photosynthesis.

The herbivorous dinosaurs also died,

As they lost their food.

The carnivorous dinosaurs could not live, either.

A great percentage of living creatures

Vanished, leaving their story,

In the layers of fossils.

After that,

Slowly, but gradually,

For a long time,

Earth repeated freezing and thawing,

Re-creating the sea and the land,

Recovering the environment,

Where life could revise.

There was no time set.

One day was the same as one thousand years.

A thousand years was one day.

Another new life began on earth.

Plants and trees re-appeared,

Together with other living creatures.

Eventually, beings that were standing on the foot

Appeared on earth.

They were later called,

Australopithecus,

Homo Erectus

Homo Neanderthal

And Homo Sapiens.

Although they look similar,

They were different from Humans.

Staying on earth for a long time,

Until they disappeared,

Just like dinosaurs vanished.

Countless kinds of creatures appeared.

All were unique on their own,

And all remained in the same forms,

Subject to slight change,

For their adaptation to the environment.

Chickens remained the chickens.

Chickens did not turn into ducks.

Goats remained goats.

Goats did not turn into lambs.

Monkeys remained monkeys.

No monkey has evolved into a human being.

Tigers were born tigers.

They never turned into lions.

All things were born and dead,

According to the law of the universe.

Every creature is unique,

Every being has its purpose,

Evolving continuously,

But not turning into another species.

Finally,

Earth formed a stable environment,

In which beings could live,

With peace and harmony with nature.

The Creator created a man in his image,

In the Garden of Eden.

As man was created in the Creator's image,

The man could create his own world,

His own environment,

According to and in harmony with

The law of nature,

Created by the Creator.

People called this time "the beginning."

It was a time when everything looked good to the Creator.

The time flew quietly.

They were not numbered.

There was day and night.

The number did not exist.

If it called a day for a day

A month is a day.

It was a time when everything was at peace.

The image of God refers to the divine nature.

The Creator has no material image.

Many people later said,

Love is the divine nature.

The common nature of all things is love.

As the creator does to the universe.

Like the process of making pottery

The creator,

For billion -folded years, like one say

Rubbed and trimmed,

For creation.

Regardless of how it was written,

The book of Genesis shows,

The course of creation

Done according to the law of the universe.

The law is the truth. The truth is love.

Love is the light.

The light is the word.

The word is life.

Heaven and earth were created,

And are being created according to the Word.

The great extinction is a part of creation,

Not a segment.

Creation gave birth to extinction.

Annihilation gave birth to creation.

Genesis says,

The man was created on the sixth day.

Do five preceding days refer to five extinctions?

With the unstable human senses,

How can man count them all?

Yet,

At least very roughly,

From one perspective,

There are two different natures.

One is absolute nature,

And the other is a relative one.

Absolute Attributes are,

A celestial thing that does not fluctuate or change,

Depending on the environment.

Divine love does not fluctuate.

Love is the axis of the universe.

Love begets forgiveness,

Forgiveness begets peace.

Love is the counterpart of the truth.

Relative nature,

Changes according to the circumstance.

The same thing could produce laughter or tears,

When it fluctuates.

All things on the earth change,

Influenced by,

and depending on the environment

This is the nature of the earth.

Earth is not eternal, therefore.

After a long time passed,

People

tried to know the origin of all things,

And the process of creation.

The creation completed,

Millions of years ago,

And the creation,

That is in the process now,

In the universe,

On earth,

And in every being.

And now too,

Thales once asked,

"What is the source of all things?"

Einstein also asked,

"How did the Creator create the heavens and earth?"

Trying to know the thought of the Creator.

Looking at the sky and the earth,

Many pondered.

Thales, Galileo, Newton, Einstein, Maxwell,

And Bohm.

These great men discovered many hidden things.

Yet,

And still,

What has been found is,

Just like a small pebble on earth,

A few tiny formulas of cosmic logic.

The truth of the universe,

It is revealed only in part,

Sometimes through observance,

Sometimes through hearing the sound,

Sometimes, through experiencing it,

And sometimes, in absolute silence,

Through the sound of silence,

Heard within.

The stars do not reveal their truth,

To the invaders.

Without invading it,

Without visiting it,

Many ancients discovered,

The truth about stars and the universe,

Through the wisdom planted within.

The great law of gravity,

It was found without invasion or visit.

Discovery that things attract the same energy,

This is also another remarkable finding,

Done without any aggression.

From ancient times,

Man looked at the sky,

Looking for the sign of the Creator,

Because of the divine nature,

The image of God,

Planted within,

From the inception,

At the time of creation.

Modern science revealed more truth.

By the principle of relativity,

With Quantum Mechanics,

Showing the macroscopic world,

And traveling the space.

Still,

Great scientists keep working,

Confessing that,

A myriad of principles exists,

In the universe,

Which man still has not figured out.

In light of that,

Everything is relative,

Except for the speed of light.

Light is the love of the Creator.

Likewise,

Only the divine love of the Creator

Is absolute and eternal.

The nature of light is life.

The reality of life,

Is unpredictable,

Until it reveals itself in some form.

Man's life is a journey through the unknown truth.

Likewise,

The order of the universe is a mystery.

In every corner of the universe,

In the valley of the universe

There is the breath of the Creator,

The unchanging law of nature,

The law of the universe,

Created with love for all.

The Letters of God

On the west side of the rocky cliff of St. Jacinto Mountain,

there are letters, letters of God.

They appear to be characters,

recorded in the ancient age.

Just like Sinai Mountain of the old days,

most of the time

the letters are covered with clouds,

hidden

like an unspeakable stone

or a silent rock.

Yet, they are texts

existing as if sleeping.

Sometimes,

very rarely,

a ray of light from the East

shakes them awake.

The clouds then slowly leave them,

making the mysterious characters

appear with stretched eyes.

The texts are hieroglyphics,

revealing themselves

only to the living and

the ones with whom they have connections.

Those letters tell a story about God,

who came to this world briefly,

wearing a human being.

They appeared to have existed,

from the time

long before a figure called Jesus appeared,

and left the earth.

Yet,

they show a figure with a thorn crown,

as if depicting Jesus wearing a crown with thorns.

That's not all.

There are,

one, in the arms of his holy mother, served by angels,

one, his birth and life as a man,

one, a crown of thorns that symbolizes suffering,

including the resurrection story.

The reason the texts are called mysterious is,

because,

each time,

depending on the observer,

they change their outer appearances.

They existed for a long time,

even before the prophecy was fulfilled two thousand years ago,

two thousand years after it was fulfilled.

Even now,

It is a record left by God.

It's a living relic.

Still,

some letters cannot be decoded.

It could be a message about an ancient time.

It could be a prophecy about the future,

about another wise man's coming.

Unknown yet,

because it doesn't give any clue.

However,

they too,

like a bride

waiting for a promised bridegroom,

as if knowing how and when they can be seen,

with eyes or with the mind,

using the light or cloud

constantly changing their shapes,

moment by moment,

they protect themselves.

The Lamentation of the East I

Oh, you, the great castle, Babel of the East,

the kings

who offered sacrifices

to the dragons in the Yellow River,

where have all gone?

A long, long time ago,

the dragons

swallowed little boys and girls,

making a legend.

They flew freely

from this world

up to the underworld,

but died in the river.

Now the stench of its carcasses

covers the sky like a fog.

Birds that lost their place,

are moaning.

Oh, how sad it is!

Oh, Balaam!

You received illicit bribes.

in secret -even unknown to God

You God hater!

You whom God is not pleased with,

you blessed the ones,

who were like the swarms of locusts,

that filled the entire field.

It's woe!

Your heart saw what you did in the dark.

You are drunk with wine,

you drank in secret.

Now you're condemned by yourself.

Barak, whom you went to find,

riding on a donkey,

is the one who sent you a delegation,

with bribes and pleasures

loaded on the carriers.

It was the beast called Isabel.

Behold!

In purple and red garments

adorned with gold and jewels,

didn't she hold a golden cup in her hand?

Oh, foolish Balaam!

Now open your ears and hear.

Listen to what the donkey

you're riding on,

has been saying.

Behold, the prince of the desert!

The one who called you

will make shiny roads in the sand desert

and the deep swamp in a jungle.

But nobody knows her intention.

O, it's woe for those who walk on the roads.

The roads are covered with silk,

She will build a grand castle beside the streets.

The magnificent artistry will be praised.

She will bribe the gatekeepers of the underworld

to enter into it,

using drones and zombies.

She will steal rare skills and treasures

which the ancient Pharaoh hid.

Then, in many luxurious ways

she'll display them as her own.

For a while, they will shine,

even at night with no stars in the sky.

Seeing the shiny light,

the merchants of the earth, young kings, pleasure–lovers

and mindless princesses

will be attracted.

She will imitate

the beautiful voice of birds.

The sweet soft voice

will tie and tie their souls.

Even the earth will get drunk

with the seducing sound.

It is such a sound of attraction

that has never been heard before.

It will not be heard elsewhere.

The sound may not be compared

to jade beads on a silver platter.

No matter how sweet it may be,

how can it be compared to her voice?

However, look, O, prince of the desert!

Finally, the sound will sting you with poison,

more toxic than a scorpion's venom.

She will push you into the snare

hidden in jungles and deserts,

that will lead you to destruction.

.

From the beginning, she was a beast.

She was the mother of a liar

who came out of Hades.

Her aiders were abominable spirits.

It is because

they also begot from the mouth of dragons.

Just like Balaam,

Those who found her,

the kings, princes, princesses

and merchants of the earth,

they will be drunken with the wine

that she gave them.

Soon

The poison will flow into their hearts.

Because,

In her room with the golden bed,

wines in the golden cup

and spices were full of poison.

An angry morning will find them.

It will shake and awake them with cruelty

Their poor bodies will scold them.

However,

the poison in their souls

still cannot be detected.

Only at that time,

they will open their eyes,

and will see her naked skin.

From a sore of the rotting flesh

and from the silk–cloak

which the beast wore

something disgusting will be oozing.

In the cup she held in her hand

were vipers and scorpions and four-legged beasts,

It was full of poison of all kinds of evil.

The cup's name is 'Rich' or 'Wealthy.'

It's just the cup

they drank from her.

All kinds of abominable spirits,

crowded to her place

to see Pharaoh's treasure.

They will laugh

because,

they have acquired

a valuable rare commodity at a low price.

The items,

she bought and sold to or from

the people and spirits

are gold and silver.

But it's a false image that will vanish,

when the light is on.

The details are in the Book of Revelation.

They are pearls, thin linens,

and purple silk clothes,

various scents, ivory,

valuable trees, grasses,

rare earth element,

lithium

wine,

refined flour, wheat, and cattle

carts, drones, zombies, ideologies

and a man's soul.

Oh, you beasts!

With all the lies and tricks and snares,

crave to covet the lands,

to enslave the thrones,

and swallow the souls of men!

The day will come

when all the merchants refuse you.

They will see the falsity of your goods

and no longer buy them.

It will be very soon.

Your goods of gold and silver

will start to stink.

The fur-scorching smell

will fill your room, castles,

and your shining splendor.

People will not look for you anymore.

They will refuse to see your cheap goods.

On the day

the kings, princes, princesses, and merchants

who committed adultery with you

will see your misery too.

The angels of death

riding on a wild wind

will be storming to you.

In the sky,

all sorts of disasters will be raining on your dead.

In fear of the troubles coming upon you

they will wail and mourn and say,

It's sad –o, a giant castle!

The days of fine linen, purples

and scarlet garments

adorned with gold jewels

and pearls are decaying.

They will be gone without any trace.

When your falsity is revealed

your false wealth also will vanish shortly.

The fire from Heaven

will burn down your dwelling place.

It will split your territory too.

People in your castle will be awakened.

Each of them will hear

the angry voices of their ancestors.

Following the voices of their ancestors,

they will raise up

the flags of their ancestors

high and high.

At the time,

Your land will tremble with the thunder sound.

The captains followed you,

the sailors who carried your goods everywhere,

those who sold their gold to you,

or those who bought your gold on credit,

will stand from a distance,

and will stamp their feet in grief.

When they see you being burnt,

they will cry out, saying

"It's sad."

There will be a voice from Heaven,

"MENE, MENE, TEKEL, PRIZIN."

From the beginning,

your righteousness did not sprout.

Your sins are piled up to heaven.

Your place

where gathered all kinds of the filthy spirits

was the haunted place,

mother of adultery.

In fact,

the wrath falling down

on your head and your back

comes out of the cups you drank.

The kings of Earth,

princes, princesses

committed adultery with you.

The merchants of the earth

slept with you.

All nations that amassed fortunes from you,

now will collapse with the wine of wrath.

The gold and silver in your storeroom,

the rare precious skills, and treasures,

were rusted and corroded.

Even nameless weeds,

blooming in the morning, vanishing in the evening

would reject your wreckage.

At that time,

Pharaohs,

who out of the underworld

will be cnraged at the treasures

that have become useless.

Those who committed adultery with her

will see their ruined figures with shame.

All the precious clothes and decorations

that have covered them

will disappear momentarily

just like a dream of a night.

They will try to find a hiding place,

without success.

Open your ears and hear.

Go away from her.

Do not make any pact with her.

Her castle is Babel.

It was built, governed, and run,

by soulless beasts.

O, my friends,

come out of there.

Don't be entangled with her.

Her sins were piled up.

Her inequities have moved Heaven,

She will face plague, famine,

griefs and ordeals.

Those who indulged in luxury,

and committed adultery with her

will wail,

beating their chests,

seeing the smoke of burning

seen in Sodom.

Woe, the great castle Babel!

The Lamentation of the East II

When the time comes,

a woman holding a kettle of water

will go to the East.

She will weep and wail

for the dead,

and for the living but dead.

O, it is lamentable!

You, the torch of the East!

If you lose your light,

you shall be thrown away.

O, remember your beginning.

it's the blood

flown out of their necks,

when their channels were cut

by the guillotine,

in the old days.

They were later called saints or martyrs.

The blood is your root.

At the time,

there was an iron wall among people.

It was among servants and lords,

cutters and the lowly,

commoners and nobles,

royals and kings.

It was the unbreakable wall

for a long time.

Confucius designed it.

Mencius executed it,

and then

The greed of nobility perfected it.

You were the one

who burnt the long-lasting iron wall.

That fire continued to burn it

for hundreds of years.

The place of ashes was your womb.

It was your beginning.

Remember the time

when the wall of inequities

stood as the wall of iron.

Remember, too,

the days of burning.

At the time

in the fire that covered the sky of night

burnt inequities.

Yet,

the inequities were not the only ones

that cried out, screaming in the fire.

The dark ghosts

who controlled people, animals,

seas and mountains

also vanished, avoiding the fire

at that very moment.

At the time,

the dark clouds disappeared, too.

For a long time,

they covered the sun,

the moon, and the stars

stopping people from looking at the sky,

from finding who they were.

In this way

greed, anger, and ignorance began to wither.

Instead,

righteousness, mercy, and faithfulness

began to sprout.

You were the pioneer who led the work.

For the first time,

people gathered on the same plane,

man and woman,

high or low

became one,

hand in hand.

O, you torch of the truth of the East,

how have you lost the precious fire

that made you the pioneer.

Now, again

the dark fogs appear,

becoming dark clouds,

soon covering the clear sky.

The blessing bestowed upon you

goes astray.

On the wall of the castle

many trunks of injustices are climbing the wall,

pushing, pulling,

and tearing off each other.

What would be your future?

Your village that used to be full of joyful singing

Is becoming ruined

by resentment,

hatred, and blames.

The front yard with laughing flowers

is turning into a barren land.

The seed of righteousness, mercy, and faithfulness

you planted at the time of burning

dried out without a trace.

O, where is the truth?

O, where is the good?

The castle that was built with the blood of martyrs

became a palace full of lies, deception, and manipulations.

All day long

from corner to corner

the sounds of accusations and tantrums overflow.

A day begins with slanders

and ends with the same.

O, the noises call for destruction!

Where is the gratitude

that was stored up in your room?

Why has it been rotten?

Why the grace of the ancestors

who spread their blood on the land

was forgotten?

Where are all the prophets and messengers

who proclaimed repentance and purification?

Why their identification cards are hanging

on a wall of a factory

manufacturing fake products,

being used as a sample for the fake ones?

Unidentifiable self-prophets

are overflowing

at stores selling counterfeits,

making noises.

How many times the Elijah

retreated and cried,

eating the bread brought by crows?

You and your land will not have rain anymore.

You claim that you can move a mountain

in the name of Jesus.

You construct a magnificent temple

with cedar trees from Lebanon.

Isn't the god you placed in your temple

an idol god you created with your own image?

Isn't that the synagogue of Satan from the start?

Hungry and thirsty

for money and people's attention,

you induce those in need to offer you

bread for their children

and drinks for their old parents.

What did they want to get from you

in exchange for the offerings?

You open the tomb,

take out the dead body,

in the name of Jesus,

proclaiming that you are a man of God.

Look closely at the one

you took out of the tomb.

He is not alive but a zombie,

that resembles you.

You threaten people

that you would remove their names

from the Book of Life kept in Heaven.

You do that in the name of Jesus.

You, a man of authority,

you made the head of the thieves, your clone

the king of the nation.

You wander all over the places,

saying that you would make dried bones revive,

with the words of the Lord.

You, a man of the holy spirit,

Look at yourself.

You are the dried bones

you are looking for.

You took a luxury place,

In the name of Jesus,

praying with screams,

until your voice gets hoarse.

You, a self-proclaimed man of prayer,

your screams for petitions

is nothing more than

the ritual of Baal's servants

who built an alter on the top of Carmel Mountain

asking for rain.

You know that

it was Elijah's prayers, not theirs,

which brought forth rain.

Your body and mind have become greasy

and oily with greed,

Not knowing that,

you shout "fire," "the fire of the Holy Spirit,"

hopping around.

The fire you are asking for

burns your invisible body,

and then your soul,

because that fire originated from Hell.

Your fire dance has no trace of holiness.

It looks very similar to

that of a ritual calling for ghosts.

The fire dance is just like

that of an ancient headsman

performed before the killing,

as a messenger of Hell.

The unrighteous apostles

Continue yelling

toward the ones with injustice.

When they open their mouths,

on the street,

the terrible odor from their stomach

is almost choking the bystanders.

Look at the donkey

who preached the word of truth

without using the name of the Lord,

on a nameless mountain,

and without the power of the Holy Spirit.

He will condemn you

just like he rebuked Balaam.

He will preach the words of God

you neglected to speak or

you trampled.

They are repentance, forgiveness,

truth, justice, love, and peace.

The candle stick is being moved.

You will see the sign.

Oh, it's woe!

The pure heart of virgin

where the Holy Spirit dwelled

now became the front yard of prostitutes.

The playground of the back mountain

is now covered with a thorn bush.

The clamorous bank of the stream

where little boys were playing

is now filled with mice,

wearing fake crowns

holding the Holy Bible

under their arms.

The farmland,

once filled with the grains for harvest

is now covered with vines of twisted arrowroots.

Grandmas, stooped for fatigue

are looking at the sky

like remnants waiting for death angels.

Where did all the brides and bridegrooms go?

In the villages,

The sweet aroma of a wedding party

stopped.

No more musical sound of flute or drum

is heard.

Nobody dances for the wedding party.

O. remember,

all kinds of traditions

declaring the birth of a baby.

When did you hear a baby's crying last?

The disappearance of a baby's crying

is an apocalypse of your future.

If you have an eye, see.

If you have an ear, hear.

The History of Gods I – The Sedona Mountain

On the peaks of the Red Rocks of Sedona Mountain,

In a place that cannot be reached or seen

Very rarely,

at the moon or star night

sages dressed in red robes appear

and play chess.

It is said,

a holy man took off his shoes of the world,

climbed up to the spot,

and saw the sages.

Most of the time

they go back

before the cracking of dawn.

Once in a while

when the sun rises

like a breathless statue,

sitting on the peak

they wait for someone else.

If they meet somebody with a connection,

without any hesitation

they're willing to speak

the wisdom of earth and heaven

even if they are not asked for it.

They said,

the theory of evolution is mistaken,

if it preaches that a human being evolved from a savage state.

According to them,

the human being was in the most auspicious time

when it was first created.

In the history of human affairs

there might have been a state of a beast.

However,

it's just a very brief chaotic moment

that was in the course of being

become fully human.

Look at what man has done!

As soon as the spirit of the Creator

is breathed into the man,

he met the Creator,

who has no form,

face to face,

talking to him.

And on his behalf,

giving all things their names,

he did please the Creator.

Despite that

there were clear instructions from the Creator

about the fruit of good and evil,

it chooses to eat the fruit against it.

From the beginning

the human being thus could not stay

as a mere gardener of Eden.

This led to the present state of human beings.

The history of gods also show

that a human being has never been savage

possibly except now.

Look at the city that was built rapidly

right after humans left Eden.

Wasn't it a magnificent place

that could be called a city of Gods?

They built splendor cities of Gods

reflecting the divinity within them.

Only by imagination alone,

as the creator did,

without any special tools

they laid the foundation on

a complicated self-made genealogy.

They created gods, and

breathed human nature into them.

They put on images to match the meaning

as Enkidu, Enill, Ananna,

Anu, Atum,

Aris, Hades,

Cronos, Zeus, - Poseidon. -

Baal, Asherah, - Molech,

They gave them fitted names and positions,

and wore immortal garments.

It was the human who entrusted them

the time and space

heaven, earth, and ocean.

everything in it,

even human himself.

The likeness of gods,

for the first time human-made,

resembled human.

It shows that, at least until then,

they were like humans in external and internal shape,

They had not been transformed into animals yet.

The image of the gods

reflected human mind

beyond the bounds of the world,

from half-man and half-beast

to scorpions and dragons,

even to the monsters of hell,

their image has changed constantly.

That is why the shape of the gods

created by humans are different,

depending on the time and place

and where they were manufactured.

The created gods could not breathe,

and most of their forms were scary and creepy.

Yet, for some reason,

the humans appeared to have forgotten that

the gods were their own handiworks.

They served the gods as if they were living,

with all their heart and soul.

They sacrificed

pigeons, sheep, cows, pigs,

and in the end, their children.

It was such an irony,

because the true God

omnipresent and omnipotent,

was very near to them, but

was invisible to them.

Humans chose to use God's name

and take its power and authority.

They clothed the idol gods with

the name, power, and authority

they took from God.

At least until then.

perhaps,

the seed of the divinity still remained,

somewhere within humans,

possibly in their subconsciousness.

They remembered,

no matter how vaguely it might be,

the name of God,

His power and His authority.

By creating gods here and there,

Humans thus tried not to turn into beasts.

The soul knew that a human could turn into a beast

If it loses the divinity within.

Because of the persistent demand of the soul,

living in each of them,

they kept making idol gods,

tricking the soul.

The road to the Eden was already blocked,

the connection was lost,

and humans could not go back,

or find the true God.

They then made fake gods as their solution,

to silence the screams of the soul.

This is how so many gods came to exist in the world.

The History of Gods II – The Sedona Mountain

Wherever there were people,

whether it's deep in the mountains

or in a palace,

wherever it might be,

gods were living luxurious lives,

wearing precious jewels,

even if many people were naked and hungry.

Dressed in immortality,

sitting in a glorious temple built by man,

were well served.

Yet,

all those gods.

at some point,

disappeared without a trace.

Those who created them,

those who worshipped them

do not know why.

It is still a mystery.

Why?

How?

Did somebody kill them all?

Did they leave humans?

In light of their splendor history,

they could not possibly be destroyed

because of a commandment:

'you shall not make for yourself an idol in the form of anything

in heaven above or on the earth beneath or in the waters below

or you shall not bow down to them or worship them.'

Considering that there is no coincidence in all things,

and that there is a cause and effect in all things,

the disappearance of the gods is a phenomenon

reflecting the humans, or

it could be a sign.

When clouds gather at the peak of a California mountain,

a mountain called a holy one by the Native Indians,

clouds signal the upcoming sandstorms.

The Hopi Indians saw signs of the phenomena of nature.

A flock of crows gathers together busily.

Suddenly

laughing flowers close their mouths.

Healing mineral waters

springing out of the hot spring well every day

suddenly stops.

A giant Cypress tree commits suicide.

All these events

might be a signal to awaken the soul,

the precious divinity within.

What would be the sign of the disappearance of all the gods?

Is it a sign of an unprecedented sandstorm?

The strong sandstorm covers the sight of a driver,

the direction of east, west, south, and north.

If so, today or tomorrow,

it might cover the realities of this world,

leading to the loss of a precious soul,

which the ancestors tried hard to avoid,

even by creating fake gods.

The History of Gods III

Even though the idols were severely criticized,

condemned by true God,

they were to be innocent.

No one could find out their fault.

Now it is revealed

what they are.

They were mere things made with

gold, silver, or stones.

They did not breathe and were fragile.

Their artistic value was trampled,

under the feet of humans many times,

But what wrongs did they do?

As true God did

they never asked for sacrifices.

nor sin offerings,

nor fellowship offerings,

nor burnt offerings.

Moreover,

they never harmed man.

No one could see their wickedness.

It was human

who placed them in cruel forms.

The one blowing fire,

out of the open mouth,

swallowing everything,

or the one with a scary human face.

In fact,

they were mere phantoms

which couldn't do anything on their own.

They were idols carved on stone,

on dust, or on wood.

Humans made them look wicked or scary

to use as their tools of threats or intimidation.

The idols themselves could not resist or defend

the humans' acts.

Since the beginning,

they were made for that purpose

as puppets for humans.

This is the tragic fate of the ones who could not breathe.

If alive,

they could take off the infamous labels on their foreheads.

The dead, however,

could not take any action to restore his reputation,

nor pay back as much as he got.

Yet,

humans' pitiful efforts in creating fake gods,

helped the humans

keep the nature of human beings

as long as possible.

By doing so, they stopped them

from turning into beasts.

At every stage of human history,

gods were thus created

in resemblance with the nature of the humans

of the time or the place.

When humans changed,

the gods changed, too.

Man-made gods' fate was

thus, in the hands of humans.

If humans cast out those lifeless gods,

they were thrown away at any time.

As time goes by,

humans stopped building temples or gods.

It might be

because people knew that

the true God

who created heaven and earth and

all things in it

has no material forms.

So, they could not deceive their soul anymore.

Today,

It is time to inscribe gods in the heart

instead of stones, wood, or gold and silver.

Thus, each man is the temple

and has his gods.

Nevertheless,

no one knows

what kind of gods

each person has in its temple.

No one can judge the gods kept in the temple

by the commandment known as

Yahweh's commandment,

Because they are hidden and invisible.

The manufactured gods,

where they are placed on

whether they are formed or not,

it would be the illusionary images

in the deep sand desert.

Keeping gods in the invisible temple

in the human mind or heart

might not be an absolute blessing.

Dark spirits can come and go

without being noticed

depending on each person's mind and heart.

Dark spirits will be invited,

when he chooses injustice over justice,

hatred over love,

vengeance over forgiveness,

resentment over gratitude.

Conscience is the divinity within.

When humans lose their conscience,

they lose their souls,

turning into human shape beasts.

A human being created with a soul,

with conscious choices

for living without conscience,

gradually turns into a soulless being,

living solely following their earthly instinct.

What else can matter more than the loss of a soul?

Once upon a time

the true God

appeared in front of man gods

to awake the sleeping souls,

and

to revive dead souls.

It was an extraordinary event

that can't be expected now.

At that time,

The manufactured gods were present

in the visible temple.

The gods were powerless,

unless humans come to the place

and called upon them.

Yet,

If the invisible idol gods

dwell in the temple of the human heart,

and if the temple becomes full of

desire to commit wrongs to others,

to steal others' rights, property, or freedom,

greed, ignorance, or wrath,

the soul, the divinity within, will lose its power,

gradually,

and then, in the end,

it may die and disappear.

If he continues to ignore the scream of the soul,

keeps serving various idols craving for more,

devotedly,

he will turn into a soulless being gradually.

The disappearance of the stone gods

is a sign of the danger humans are facing.

.

The History of Gods IV

It's not only light and darkness

falling from Heaven.

Among many,

the story of the three Magi from the East

shows a treasure falling from Heaven.

While looking at the stars in the sky,

the Magi picked up the secret treasure map.

From the beginning,

this way, that way,

the Heaven,

put a bug in people's ears

about small or big events

to be taking place on Earth.

In fact,

questions and answers about the meaning of life

have been dawning down like drew

in the silent night from Heaven,

while everybody is asleep.

A long time ago,

the sages, being wet with night dews,

with pure heart,

were united with the night as one.

The questions the sages indulged in

were passed on to others,

more and more,

continuously.

Thanks to this,

people came to question

who they were,

why they came to the world,

and the meaning of life,

trying to find a way to become true humans.

Some started a long pilgrimage,

looking for the traces of invisible gods.

No matter what might have happened to each of them

during the course of the pilgrimage,

whether they met gods or not,

whether they found the answers to their questions,

their initiations

and their journeys

are their efforts to remain humans.

However,

the gods they might meet

through pilgrimage

could not give answers to the questions,

as those gods are man-made,

not breathing.

Still,

these seekers might find their true selves.

which were hidden,

through the journey,

not through the breathless idols,

on their own.

It's vanity.

Seekers who started a journey

looking for treasures from gods

will come back empty-handed,

as real treasures cannot be found

in the relics of idols' temples.

Humans should not be seduced

to be ignorant,

by void ideas, propaganda,

gold, or treasures,

far from the real truth.

Rather than creating idols with stones,

many are trying to be self-made idols,

Transforming into beasts.

Cutting off a final trace toward the way,

choosing to abandon their souls,

inducing others to the same path,

they choose to be fake Gods.

Human idols revive the old dead rituals,

demanding worship, blood offerings,

hymns and human sacrifices.

They no longer have questions

or curiosity

about the meaning of life,

If they can find a pure, living water

in which they can see their souls

reflected,

it will be a historical blessing.

A lucky one might see,

surprisingly,

a bizarre creature in the water,

which he has never seen.

It will be tough,

or impossible for anyone

to accept that the horrible thing is himself.

It took a long time

for a human shape to turn into an ugly creature.

Yet,

It's not over.

He still can choose to restore

a beautiful lost soul.

It might take the same long time.

As he is still human,

his choice will open a door

leading to the way toward healing.

Who will bring the mirror

that may reflect the soul,

and give it free,

to those walking on the path of beasts?

Who will hold their hands,

leading them to human status

that is vanishing into the air?

Who will supply food for the soul,

leading to life?

Who will bring the living water,

which will eradicate the eternal thirst?

Who will heal the leper's lesion?

He himself is the healer.

Only he can cure the lesion.

Only he can seek and find

the living water and food for his soul.

These are the words of sages

who came down

on Sedona Mountain.

The voice is, however,

is from his inner self, his own soul.

It could be the last will of his soul,

which may not be heard,

if he had already turned into a soulless being.

Epilogue - The Chosen Destiny

The yearning-like blossoms of plum

Stay dead.

As time goes by,

It becomes oblivion.

When the time comes,

The lifeless oblivion,

Being melt,

Is arising as a foam of longing,

Turning into the cloud.

The cloud dies,

Being transformed into the rain.

When the rain stops falling,

The cloud appears again.

Longing is not the only one,

That is repeating living and dying,

And arising from death.

In the darkness,

The light appears dead,

Without any trace of memory.

Yet looking closely,

It still is living,

Like a dormant volcano,

That might arise,

Abruptly and unexpectedly.

Blooming in nature,

Disappearing in nature,

Repeating living and death,

That is a constant cycle.

Huge cloud, a small cloud,

Beautiful, ugly,

Whatever form it may be,

Looking closely,

Rain becomes a cloud,

Cloud becomes rain,

Changing only in form.

Whether it is considered notable or invisible,

The ending of any life is the departure from earth.

The meeting becomes parting,

The parting becomes a meeting,

Life meets death,

Death meets life,

Changing in form,

Constantly, as always.

I don't know if it is dead or alive,

if it is good or evil,

Or if it is virtue or sin.

All are in one.

All are changing unceasingly.

Milton Keynes UK
Ingram Content Group UK Ltd.
UKHW050203010823
426090UK00003B/66

9 781803 697475